All the Lies
I Tell Myself

CHELSEA TRUE

Copyright © 2020 Chelsea True
All Rights Reserved.

Year of the Book
135 Glen Avenue
Glen Rock, PA 17327

Print ISBN: 978-1-64649-106-3
Ebook ISBN: 978-1-64649-107-0

No part of this publication may be reproduced, distributed, or transmitted in any form or by any means, including photocopying, recording, or other electronic or mechanical methods, without the prior written permission of the publisher, except in the case of brief quotations embodied in critical reviews and certain other noncommercial uses permitted by copyright law. For permission requests, write to the publisher at the address above.

To Zoë & Chase – the true great loves of my life,
who continue to inspire me to be more every single day.

And to all the brave and broken hearts
that continue to love and dream,
long after all seems lost.

Contents

All the Lies I Tell Myself	1
Denial	4
Phoenix Fire	6
Complicated	7
Storms	8
Chapter Break	9
Sand	10
Ships	11
Thoreau	12
The Gray	15
Northern Lights	16
The Deep	18
Illusions & Mirrors	20
Faith	23
Circles	25
Blinders	27
New	31
Hotel Rooms	32
Just Us	34
Everything I Need	36
Black Lace	37
You	38
Poker	39
Arguments	41
Puzzles	42
Destruction	44

Ghosts	45
Pandora's Box	46
One Night	48
Con Artist	49
Enigma	51
I Know Better	54
Haunted	55
Darkness & Light	56
Bottled Words	58
Wanderer	59
Our Chapter	62
Acceptance	63
Tower of Babylon	64
Humpty Dumpty	65
The Middle	66
Victims	67
Memories	68
Bleach	69
A Moment in Time	70
Once in a While	72
Cobwebs & Boxes	73
Raindrops	76
Castle	77
Life & Death	80
All That Remains	82
Open Road	84
Respite	85
Backroads & Eternity	87
Sirens	90
Resting Place	91
Someone to Choose Me	92

Death Among the Trees	94
Old Friend	95
Beautiful & Broken Things	96
The One	97
Halves to My Heart	98
Last Call	100
A Chance of Storms	102
Dreams	103
Simple Things	104
Twilight	105
Midnight Circus	106
Flash Flame	109
World Eater	110
Unlikely Companions	112
New York	114
Lost & Found	117
Oceans	120
Loneliness of a Friend	121
Strange Times	124
Letting Go	126
Metamorphosis	128
Home	130
Free	132

All the Lies I Tell Myself

All the lies
we tell ourselves,
the little untruths that fall
into the cracks of
our insecurities,
to giant falsehoods we write into
our own histories
so we can finally sleep at night.

I wish I was better,
I wish you were better, too.
But wishes don't make up
the foundations that lives need,
they only sound
pretty by starlight
and dissolve in the
harsh reality of dawn.

We are simply human,
thus, we lie
and we love.
We ache and
we yearn.

We are not black and white,
but vast and gray.
It is between all the lines
that you and I seem to fall.

Perhaps the most honest
we have ever been
is in the harsh
art of our felt pain,
drawn into the
tapestry of our lives
that we later rewrite,
etched in sorrow,
purchased in tears,
tattooed on our souls.

Your truth
and my truth…
they never align.
Perhaps that is the
fallacy of love,
that each version
becomes our unique history,
coloring the past,
changing the landscape
of our future.

I'll wish you well…
and more love and light
and happiness.
Alas, the great lies
we continue to tell ourselves,
immense and soul-consuming.

Better to pretend,
white-out the ugly reality
than to deal with
all the could-have-beens,
the heavy weight of mistakes,
the loss of a far better
and different story
than the one we are now
forced to tell.

The lies...
the half-truths...
they are what break us,
unseen by anyone but ourselves,
and yet,
conversely they are all
that make us
exactly what we are.

Denial

Your soul is like your poetry,
beautiful and unbalanced,
a little astray and contradictory.
Complex and self induced,
full of love and light
and ageless mystery.

You say you want only to see silver linings
and focus on the hope.
You choose to blame the storm clouds in your life
on chance and history as a way for you to cope.

You tilt reality's glass in the sunlight until
you get
the refracted rainbow that you seek.
Lovely and slight false,
distorted just enough to quiet your mind
so you can finally get some sleep.

Wounds that you ignore don't heal
unless you lance them,
leaving scars that won't ever fade.
You can't ever rebuild foundations
unless you can acknowledge to yourself
all the things you unmade.

Ensconced in your denial,
you drown out the doubts with self talks
and good intentions.

So focused on the need to be right
that you lose all the true answers to
all the right questions.

You seem caught in your imposed stasis,
you willingly choose to mistake
accountability for pessimism so you can ignore
the wreckage in your wake.

You get lost in your own story,
all my words are just white background noise.
Some things you cannot talk into being,
no matter how hard you try or the methods
you employ.

So do I just wish you well,
my love,
and quietly read the novel that you write?
Stay silent and unassuming,
let you continue to wonder why we both
sleep alone at night?

For while you were pouring out
your distorted pages,
you will look up one day soon and find
that all we could have been is now lost
in scars and splinters,
wondering how you could be so blind.

Phoenix Fire

I am not an open book
you can rifle through
when the dark and the loneliness consumes you,
when your thoughts get too loud and you need a
distraction from the noise.
I have a fire,
always raging and aching inside of me...
But I am better at scorching bridges right now
than
I am at tearing down walls.
You'll have to come and find me
when the lights are low and
let me see something real in your eyes.
Search for me in the hollow hideaways of the
world,
phoenix flames and
burning bright.
Scale these walls,
taste my mystery,
and maybe, just maybe
find something true with me.

Complicated

I am not for everyone,
I am not beautiful or graceful or safe.
I am not a lazy weekend morning or
a quiet autumn sunset.
I am a 3 AM on a work night,
a broken window in the dead of winter,
the itch in the center of your back
you just can't seem to reach.
I fall from modern ideals with a dull thud,
and trip over invisible barriers on the street.
I apologize for my awkward sadness and
my paradox of asking
profound questions before coffee
but won't respond to simple things.
I wonder sometimes if I don't belong around people,
if I was made more for
patterned leaves and dappled sunbeams
and the shadows in between.
All that darkness
and that light
mixing together underneath the
surface of my skin,
creating squalls and chaos,
lightning storms and mystery.
I'll always be the misunderstood magic
that most people fear and run from,
and yet,
also the simplest truth that they all
unknowingly seek.

Storms

I can't hear anything over the screaming
in my head,
a tsunami of thought,
all roar and salt and darkness.
How do you outrun what is inside you?
All that I am is roiling in waves,
writhing in familiar agony,
tossing in a pointless fear...
that I am not any wiser than I once was.
My past is a litany of riptides,
caught forever in the ebb and pull of
careless hands and empty hearts.
Just a wall of water and undercurrents,
taking me further out to sea.
I don't want to drown here,
but I can't seem to find the air
I know I need to breathe.

Chapter Break

Tasted the dawn air,
hinting of rain,
salty with dew.
Felt like I might just
keep on running,
past all thought and memory,
lose it all in the misty light,
rebounding off the sharp edges
of this sleepy little town and the
blinding windshields of
early morning commuters.
The sun struggling to break free
of its blanket of cloud,
trying to kiss the tops of
frosted trees,
warm rays and heightened shadows.
Maybe this isn't the end of the story,
lost in the fog of an early spring.
Sunrise makes you believe
the story hasn't truly ended,
that perhaps moments like these
are merely just a chapter break.

Sand

Little grainy worlds
caught and crushed
between my toes.
Scattering and combining
with the salt and the sea.
Puffs of sand in mini explosions
beneath the waves,
swirled with ocean foam.
Mother Nature's expert cocktail,
I drink it all in deep.
I take it straight,
riding high on simple rolls of water
that transform into murky sheets
of glass in the curled aftermath.
I am shattered and remade with
each ebb and flow,
pebble rocked and dark.
I am lost to the tides of time,
awash forever in memory.

Ships

Are we just passing ships in the night,
close enough to see a glimpse of each other's lights,
a brief interlude from a lonely voyage,
a quick illusion of connection
before the long night closes in?
I wish you could just come on over,
climb aboard these hulls,
and take my helm and
steer me back to you.

Thoreau

Mists of dawn slowly rising
like the lifting of Morning's underskirt,
revealing secrets and beauty
painted in sunlight and shadows,
inspiring a desperate desire
for the quiet and a nameless peace.

Pebbled rocks and wet earth
at my feet,
the constant chatter of the stream flows
like an endless white noise
inside my head,
drowning out the ugliness
of my thoughts of late.

The wildness of these backwoods
and the taste of summer in the air
camouflage sins and failures alike,
allowing me to detox slowly
this time,
from the oft self inflicted wounds
that I can't seem to avoid
no matter how hard I try.

The gift that keeps giving,
the scars that won't heal,
I keep endlessly choosing people
and places
that only hurt me.

Only to despair over the
exhaustion of my soul anemia,
love and life leaking out
of lacerations and lesions,
soundless and percolating,
leaving me mostly
empty and dry.

Is all that I am simply never enough,
or is it rather that the people
I let look behind the curtain
lack something vital and needed
to decipher
all the glittering angles of
my heart
and decode the encrypted
volumes of my soul?

The hushed wisdom of these trees
whisper knowledge to me
in the sway of their
dew-studded branched arms,
clothed with June leaves
and ancient truths,
yet their words get lost to me
in the distance of the air.
My soul goes a little astray
in the din of moving water
and the hum of the forest.

I am so tired these days,
bone-deep and world weary,
I ache for the void
of a dreamless sleep.
Perhaps for a few years,
at least long enough to wake up
past the pinpoints of pain,
all skin and muscle and
spirit numbed and
devoid of sensation.

So I stay here,
comforted by water and earth and sky,
blanketed in nature,
hidden from the world outside,
to sleep away the suffering
until I can greet the rising Sun
and her petticoats of mist
with more than known questions
and self prescribed misery.

I'll rest until
I am more
or maybe finally,
everything
and everyone else
will all be less.

The Gray

The sky is gray,
slate-colored and vast.
Undefined and lasting,
no mirrored sun reflected on
the horizon's glass.

My feet are always moving,
dogged and resiliently steadfast.
Most days I can't tell if
I am running towards a future,
or simply escaping the past.

The sky is stone and smoke,
dull and empty,
merely weak sunlight and
muted sound.
No inspired landscapes here,
only a soul canyon where all these
doubts echo and rebound.

Now I too am colorless and ashen,
hesitant and unsure,
unmoving on this now uncertain ground.
For surely the loneliest thing to be
is me, lost,
endlessly waiting to be found.

Northern Lights

I find myself at a crossroads,
one foot in a house of fire,
the other in a world of ice.
I can choose to continue
to blaze,
or let it all go and
encase myself in winter.

I find the longer
I am on this earth
and the more I see of people,
that I will gladly
choose the cold
and its subsequent numbness
than the flash and flame
of love and lust
that turns quickly to ash
long after the heart
continues to burn.

So please stop trying
to ignite the embers
of what once was,
I willingly choose the frost.
All pain deserves to be felt,
but I find I am at
the threshold for yearning
for what cannot be and loss.

I choose the frozen wasteland
of all memory
and a broken landscape
of what we were
over the pyre of more lies
you sell
and a feeling, bleeding heart.

The aurora borealis
of my memory,
lovely and distant,
plays across my broken
and chilled love.
And I find that is enough
to sustain and protect me
from any further harm.

Beautiful and lonely,
all that has once been
and ever was,
once longed for and lost,
become my own
Northern Lights
across my broken stars.

The Deep

Sometimes I need to leave
the words on the page,
sometimes I need to just walk away
and let the ink settle in.
Let my emotions dry and fade into the paper,
close and lock the door
to the chasm of my soul for a while.

I need to dampen the flames and
embrace the quiet that only comes
with the veritable distance I create
away from all the questions and
the poetry still left inside of me.

I could drown in those bottomless waters,
all love and loss and pain,
all brine and salt and sea.
I'll find a way to stay afloat
with compartmentalizing
and denial,
I'll become buoyant with shallow emotions
and wasted air.

Arms and legs outstretched,
lungs burning with held breath,
body and spirit now numb with
all the hidden depths
and the incessant cold.

I'll fix my eyes on some distant shoreline
or maybe simply
the long, endless shape of the horizon,
lovely and lonely
and far beyond my reach.

And here I'll remain,
away from the dark paint and unwritten pages,
until perhaps something
or someone
far greater than myself
pulls me away from
the silence and the solitude.

Down into all the penned words and written
lines
and emotions that won't sleep...
once more I'll go,
below the surface and the superficial,
down into the deep.

Illusions & Mirrors

I want to shatter all the mirrors in the world,
silence the voices in my head that
pour malice in my brain,
pinpointing and magnifying all my flaws
until they are all I see.
I want to cut away skin,
redraw my entire design.
I am filled with equal parts of dull despair
in the apparent unloveliness of my reflection,
and in the pointless waste of my energy,
wishing for a perfection that I can never have.

Feeling foolish for longing for
such shallow and empty things.
Not even for myself,
but for you.
So maybe then I can be the only thing you see.
Maybe then I could be enough
to keep you close to me.
But I don't have the funds for a surgeon
scalpel
nor enough pills in the world
that can make me closer to the strange ideals
all men seem to seek.

So instead I'll drink another glass of wine
and turn off the lights,

and we can both pretend for a bit
to be something we wish we could be.
You can paint over my imperfections
with your ignorance in the dark,
and I can imagine you as someone better,
who finds my soul more beautiful
and important
than superficial eyes can see.

But don't worry, love,
I'll make sure to leave long before
the dim rays of dawn
highlights all the broken edges of me
and the faded lines of my long lost makeup
and the insecurity that wraps around me
like a gray cloak of loneliness,
both sheltering and isolating.

You can say all the pretty lies
but the truth is there in your closed eyes,
here in these moments in the night.
I will always be just a blank vessel you lose
yourself in from time to time,
different faces and bodies running in your
mind.
It's okay...
Empty yourself into me,
like always,
and I'll leave before
the dawn breaks like a yolk
on last night's dinner plate.

A dull shadow fading away
in the morning mist,
before you see the knowledge on my imperfect
face
and feel the genuine sadness in my touch.
You will forget me by the time you begin
your AM rituals,
lost in the fantasies that will heat your blood
but inevitably kill your soul,
distorted visions from a safe distance
that don't require you to try or care.

Perhaps you will feel
a vague recollection of a momentary relief
and a small sense
that maybe you misplaced something precious
somewhere in between
the fade of sleep and
your early morning coffee beans.

Faith

I keep searching for You
but all the dark and tangled tendrils of me
get in my own way.
I know You are
the beginning and the end,
and yet, I still can't seem to find You.

Is that You whispering throughout the
endless hour that I can't hear
over the raucous din of my life?
Was that Your touch I felt when
I was alone,
weeping in the dark?

I am lost,
wandering down a path I chose
but didn't truly want.
Come find me...
Because I find that
I don't know the way back
to You.

I am weighted with stones,
shiny, heavy gems of Shame
and Guilt
and Regret.
I am shackled
by my own arrogance and selfishness,
determined for independence,

always knowing what I want,
but never what I need.

I am heavy,
stuck on a pattern I can't seem to disrupt.
I am weary.
I am broken.
Do You see me?
For surely no one else seems to.

Lighten my burden...
Please...
Come find me
or I fear that I will
forever be lost.

Circles

You talk of endings and beginnings,
starts and finishes.
My world is made of circles...
a groundhog day of hopes and mistakes that
I keep on replay.

A midnight glance across a crowded room and
you find me here,
caught in a stasis,
desperately longing to shut down the careening
carousel of me...
to get off this ride and stagger toward some
rabbit trail with no destination,
just roads of the lovely unknown.

You touch me and the spinning falters in the
strange and yet familiar taste of you.
I can't see or feel the difference
in the whirling now,
I have tunnel vision,
I see only you.
But I am still circling,
still caught in your loop and mine.
If I leapt off now,
would we shatter?
Broken little what-ifs and could-have-beens
littered on your apartment floor like our clothing?

Or would we instead find sturdy ground and
a hand to hold?
Could we break pattern and find something
lasting, rare and real?
Or are we just passengers on a train to nowhere,
sitting side by side,
killing the loneliness and quieting the memories
for a brief time?

I can't seem to stop myself from giving
tiny fragments of me away,
leaving fractured breadcrumbs that lead back
to some vulnerable ember in that circle of me...
I don't know myself if I want you
to fan me back to life or
stamp the last, stuttering flame of me out.

I let you read all the broken veins of me
on and beneath my skin,
but draw away when I hear
the truth of it on your lips.
Maybe I am doomed for circles...

Round and round, I go...
Wanting someone to save me,
make the world stop spinning for a while.
But it's me...
Just me.
Lost forever on this carousel ride.

Blinders

He says he wants to see...
but then he says a lot of things.
I can stumble through his language,
though I am not prone to over the top ways
or monetary means.

Yet somehow he never seems to be able
to decipher all the lines of me.
I know I'm not an easy read,
I've got ironies and dichotomies
written all over my pages,
whole chapters that even I keep
under careful lock and key.

I still really only ugly cry in showers,
and hide my marks and scars
with cheap cream and high-priced sarcasm,
powered by trauma and
large doses of caffeine.

He talks about communication,
but blindly misses open doors
and real vulnerabilities.
He disappears after dark most nights,
and only seems to call
when he knows that I'm not free.

He's played the Game so long,
changing rules and rewriting history,
that he has forgotten that
no one collects at 'Go' here,
that there are no real winners
when it comes to Make Believe.

And I know better than most
what blinders feel like,
how easily one can mistake
delusions for reality,
the drug high-low ecstasy
of pain mistaken for
True Love's misery.

How sometimes we can get
so desperate to feel
Something,
Anything...
that we'll take a hit from another
lonely heart,
lying to ourselves
that it has to mean
Something...
Anything.

I still find myself there,
dark alleys of memory,
long empty streets of a
nameless need.

So while I have the boundless grace and
all the miles of desired empathy,
it doesn't change
a single damn thing
about what I want
or the warnings I should heed.

All the tiny ways that
a love can die,
little gray unseen deaths.
For all love brightens,
leaving hollows and long shadows
in its wake...

He blames it on odd things,
because he doesn't carry my ink
on his back
or that he refuses to drink
his morning coffee black,
like the type of men that
I usually see.

But the truth is he is so busy
building his own version of
a castle in the sand,
that in the end
there is just no room for me...

The only place left is
Watching and
Waiting,
away from his forlorn shore.
Alone,
I am in the deep
and the dark,
in the rise and the fall,
in the black and endless surge
of the lost and aching sea.

New

You saw me in a way
I can hardly fathom,
not shattered like a broken vase
but rather a mosaic made from
fragmented glass and held
together by memory,
reflecting a rainbow of
love and light
into your eyes.

Hotel Rooms

I wake up to bold lines of sunlight
escaping from the edges of
the long blinds that I hastily
closed in the early hours
of the morning,
when we stumbled in like drunkards
and collapsed among the sheets.
I want to stay in the dark
where our secrets can live
and breathe,
where the black edged shadows
of your outline and
the alcohol tinged
taste of your tongue
beckons me
down long corridors
of want and need.
Curtains closed,
I crawl back to you,
escaping the reality
of sunrise and all its questions,
by getting lost in the warmth
of your resting skin
and your hair that falls on
my face.
These moments
are everything
and yet never enough,

lasting and
yet short-lived.
You try to hide in the blankets,
and tell me to stop staring,
but I can't do anything
other than look at you.
You fill my vision.
I need to snapshot
you in this moment,
perfect and tousled,
your skin contrasted with my own,
darkness and light.
So, love, let me...
Let me memorize the curve of your smile
and the wild disarray of your hair
and the salt and sweetness of the
curve of your shoulder where
it meets your neck.
Let me pretend that we'll
have a thousand more of these moments,
even though we both know
the fingers of dawn
creeping across the hotel room floor
signal the end of all things.

Just Us

Looking at you
looking at me...
Barely a breath between us
and yet an ocean of other lives lies between.
Your lips are warm
but the tip of your nose is cold,
alas, always the
fire and ice of you.
Your taste of mellowed wine mixes with my
late afternoon coffee,
all the bitter and
all the sweet,
jumbled together until it's just hot air.
Yours,
Mine,
Ours.
I want to show you me and
I want to disappear.
I want everything and nothing,
all at the same time.
Somehow the enigma of you has
soaked into my skin,
made me contrary and unsure.
I draw you in against my better judgment,
you smell of shaving cream and early winter.
I need you to ignore the racing of my heart
that I know we both can hear,
let's just blame it on the caffeine.

Please don't try and take
what I don't have left to give anyway.
Just lay for a moment in the quiet.
Just you,
Just me,
Just us.

Everything I Need

The smell of your soap and
the sound of the air moving through your lungs and
the touch of your skin against mine and
the taste of your lingering on my tongue...

These things are all I need,
they are the breath and life of me.

Black Lace

You touch,
I quake.
You taste,
I shake.
I burn,
You take...

I end,
You begin.
I breathe out,
You breathe in.

The whole world
narrowed to here,
this time,
this place.
Just you and I,
rumpled sheets
and lovely satin
trimmed in black lace.

You

Tossing and turning,
sleep eludes me now...
this constant running of my mind
keeps me prisoner,
wearing me down.
I turn and see your shadowed face,
match my breathing to your exhales,
trace the dips and lines of your body,
let your heated skin soak into the coldness
of my own.
All the fears,
all the worries
disappear when I am filled to the brim with you.
You are the answer
to all the questions.
You are the quiet of the storm
inside of me.

Poker

You say it's simple,
Love just is.
But I think Love is like a house of cards
made of spun glass,
intricate and complex,
refracting and reflecting shadows and light.
Often wondering how it remains standing when
even the air wants to test its boundaries
and barriers and fragile strength.
How do you build something lasting
out of broken parts,
hairline fractures and almost invisible fissures
running like scars throughout both
you and I?
Could we fill those seams with wild hope and
forgotten dreams until they become
crossroads of gold,
mapping out our histories until our card tower
burns like melted amber and crystal,
tawny and tarnished,
gilded and glimmering,
balanced only on sharp edges and
unspoken promises?
Or do we just pick amongst our rubble,
choosing a few nicked and splintered pieces
to play a round or two,

using sleight of hand tricks and
the angle of the fading light to make us out to be
more than we ever were?
I don't think my brittle and marred Queen
can beat your damaged King,
but then Loneliness always comes in
like an Ace on the river,
and beats the House anyway.
Do we rise, steadfastly and painfully,
placing in piece by jagged piece,
a potential masterpiece of
stained glass in the twilight,
perchance to fall and shatter
from far greater heights?
Or do we check and balance ourselves,
choose to fold long before the end,
safe away from the edge of
either true oblivion or joy?
I don't even know if I have the currency
to play your table stakes anymore…
So maybe all we are now is another what-if
to add to our own rivets of burnished gold,
solitary rivers of shimmering regret that
run unseen beneath
our faded and mirrored skin,
wishing for another chance
to beat the odds
and have just one more
hand to play.

Arguments

Always on the offense,
you never give any ground, regardless
of what is false or what is true.
What is it you are so afraid of?
That I might actually see into
the vulnerable heart of you?

Your vision is set,
all black and white lines.
Control will always be your drug of choice.
But my world has always been gray,
and in these moments,
I find I still have no power,
no voice.

My walls and defenses
have been chipped away by
my foolish love for you...
I wish you could take a little more care,
a few misplaced words can break us,
sharp syllables tinged with black and blue.

I try to give you reasons,
even now in the bloody aftermath,
I try to see it through.
But you always leave me with empty promises and
a loss that remains both achingly familiar
and yet somehow new.

Puzzles

Painted dusk and motion pool lights
hide half your face in shadow.
I have never had much patience for puzzles,
but something in your gaze
makes me want to stay.

In this moment,
I am not sure if it is the wine
or you that makes me a little
unsteady on my feet.
You taste of secrets
and tannins,
of baked summer nights
and forbidden things.

Though the touch of your
unfamiliar hands calls to the
deep in me,
there is something
infinitely more lost
in your eyes.
And as my compass
was broken long ago
by harsh hands and
wayward hearts,
I can't find you here.

So I'll pack up empty glasses
and keep anything from
falling out of my chest
and landing in an offering at your feet.
I'll wish you well and mean the words.
But decide to keep
all that remains
of my mystery,
locked away
for only me.

Destruction

You are the tread,
I am the flower.
You are the thunder,
I am the cower.
You only leave destruction
in your wake.
Please let me go,
for both of our sakes.

Ghosts

Here you go again...
offering me everything,
and I hesitate.
I am still haunted
by ghosts.
They find me in odd moments
and remind me of
lost things,
all I have given away.
I don't know quite what
to do with you...
You're perfect
but you're not him.
That's part of why I love you
and also why you'll never
be enough.
A soul can't live in
two different times at once,
you have to choose between
where you have been
and what lies ahead.
Courage fails me now,
so I stumble and trip
into the past,
choosing to stay among the
phantoms of history
instead of moving on.

Pandora's Box

I taste them on your lips,
I feel them in your touch.
You call them Pandora's box,
I call them other things...
You make them more than just scars,
your brokenness somehow cuts into me,
blood on blood,
a strange cocktail of conjoined,
insecure misery.
Your unfettered words
never stop the bleeding,
tongue tied and soul sick,
I empty myself until I am
but a shell
of who I was before I loved you.
You wear glasses of shame and guilt,
you can't see past your own darkness
to see me.
I fade in,
I fade out.
Alas, I am invisible again.
All I wanted was to be kept
in your chest pocket,
next to your heart,
constant and steady,
ticking away the years together.
But you never bothered with
stitches or apologies,

so you lost me somewhere,
though you don't know
where or why or when.

One Night

Lost myself somewhere in the distance to you.
You taste of salt and moonlight and a hint of regret.
Can we stay here, tangled in bedsheets
and trepidations and
starlight?
Blazing with the heat of skin to skin,
tasting of the unknown,
cocooned by the night?
I'll whisper all my secrets to you
and let you see a glimpse
of truth in my touch.
We can let our bodies exchange
what our voices dare not say,
and when the morning comes,
we can put our nonchalance on with our clothes
and speak of the weather.
We'll part ways as strangers,
and pretend we don't feel a loss.

Con Artist

You read me someone else's lines,
but always only after midnight.
Eloquent and lonely,
maybe we were only made for the inky dark
and the starlight.

You describe emotions and create labels,
entire worlds in your head,
outlined in mist and dreams.
Eyes straight forward, never glancing back,
I see the lost boy hidden there,
coming apart slowly at the seams.

Maybe it's those small truths I see or
maybe because you hide the brokenness
a little too deep, a little too well…
But as I relearn the lines of me,
patching up the rusted clockwork of my heart,
I find I don't want the phantoms you sell

I want to kiss away all your frown lines
and quiet the spiraling highway of your brain,
far too loud and all-consuming.
Sometimes I can barely see past the current hour,
but somehow you get lost in the future,
always unknown and forever looming.

The greatest lies we tell are often to ourselves,
about who we are, what we use to fill
the endless chasm inside.
Each of us no better or worse,
simply human facing each dawn,
choosing our masks and the demons we hide.

Your voice is laced with sincerity and
I innately feel in the echoes that
you truly care for me.
But I also don't believe you sleep alone,
that you keep the tendrils of emptiness at bay
with secrets chained where no one can see.

I'll ache to give you some small parts
that ease away your sadness...
tiny refracting rays of light through the haze.
But you'll never get to the heart of me
with untruths,
it remains lost, waiting to be found,
forever and perhaps always.

Enigma

Sometimes I still long
to understand your words.
In weak moments,
I wish it was for me
that you still write.

But perhaps,
most of the time,
I am too old
or just too damn tired
to play pretend with myself
anymore.

Still, the enigma
and the beauty of your soul
has always called to me.
Art to art,
loneliness to loneliness,
quiet strength and yet,
the deep fear of ever
being truly known.

I wish I could see,
I could touch,
I could lighten the darkness
that seems to shadow
us all.

There was a time when that need
mattered more than air,
more than breath,
more than it should.

But now,
I find I am the one who
desperately needs to be seen,
to be felt,
to be wanted more than logic
dictates I should.

So while your words will always
light a fire in me,
a need to know and understand
all the shadows and light of you,
I am more.

And yet... still...
perhaps I am still less.
For under the grown mask that I wear
and all the lies that I tell myself,
alone in the dark,
I will always long for you
to seek me,
to desire me enough
to want to learn the dawn and midnight of me,
hidden away in black lace
and forgotten needs.

All the poetry I have yet to know
and write,
forming words and sound and life,
somewhere in the space between
my beating heart
and the brain that knows better
of me.

I Know Better

Somehow I always end up here...
lost in my desire for you and
all the impossible things.
I can't even blame you anymore,
because I know you now.
I see all the broken, jagged edges
of you,
and yet,
I still keep blindly cutting myself
and then wonder why
I am always bleeding out,
hollowed and empty.
Love is a madness
when it comes to you and I...
I don't want to live in these
four white walls of us
anymore,
but I can never seem to leave.

Haunted

Keep getting lost in what once was...
instead of what now is.
Tripping over nostalgia into cracks
of memory,
losing the path back to reality in the
shrouded fog of you.
Cobwebs of thoughts and longings
clinging to my skin,
thinner than bands of sunlight,
stronger than bone.
I am covered by our history,
I am shadowed in ghosts.
Every page of me has been
written on in permanent ink by you...
I wish I could tear out some of the pages,
start parts of our story over again,
and rewrite all the broken lines.

Darkness & Light

I see you...
here in these moments,
past - future - present...
they all collide into
the slice of seconds,
out of time,
when I look into your eyes.
Your sadness calls to my sadness,
your darkness and my darkness,
searching for a light in one another.
Together could we create a sun or
would we just go into deeper and darker shadows
than we knew alone?
If we combine skin to skin,
will we create all flame and beauty?
Or make just one more skeleton to add
to the hidden closet of all our past mistakes?
Maybe we are both a little lost,
stumbling around in the night,
palms outstretched,
seeking contact of any kind.
An innate need to be found,
to be seen and known.
But I am drowning in questions,
I am sinking in doubt.
You bring your lips to my lips,
you muddy up the running waters of my fears.

Which way is up,
which way is down?
I am solely surrounded
by the dense mystery of you.
Your fingers are tattooing secrets
on my skin,
taking in your inked marks
and bleeding out small pieces of me.
Until all that remains are
echoes of past and present,
held together by
something stronger than pain,
deeper than words.
So stumble through the dark with me,
my love,
and together maybe we can make
our own brilliant light.

Bottled Words

I wrote your name in the sand,
cursive and long lined.
I watched the tide take you away.
I poured my heart into a green glass bottle,
airtight with all the words
I can't seem to say.
I tossed it out,
far beyond your wake,
lost and floating and free.
Vulnerable to currents and storms
and all the monsters
of the deep and lonely sea.

Wanderer

You wander in and out of my life
like a mist,
gray and mysterious and
impossible to hold.
The angsty lone wolf,
the artistic cowboy
with life-carved hands and
bottomless eyes.

You are transient and lovely,
lonely and set apart.
You and I always on the fringes
of a far too crowded and voyeuristic society,
we are always somehow falling
into the cracks of this world.

I used to think of you as untethered but with
a core that was constant and true,
even if I carry a few scars that might
say otherwise from you.
But if Time has taught me nothing else these
long years,
it's that I don't know a damn thing about
another's soul or what's inside them,
what hills of thought they're willing to die on,
or what they'll break or build
with words and hands and actions.

And yet,
even now,
in a cloud of forgotten cigarette smoke and
hazy memory,
my blood remembers the fire of yours when it
caught with mine.

You can't stay,
you never do,
but maybe my world is just a little too cold
in the dark of this January night.
It might just be worth another unseen
white-lined constellation on my heart
to get a little lost,
for a moment,
in the constant heat and solitude of you.

Mountain trails and
river campfires,
sawdust and ashes,
morning coffee and country tunes,
there will always be traces of you,
from time to time,
in these penned lines of mine.

Maybe, if I'm lucky,
you can think of me on certain winding roads or
when a certain song comes on the radio.
And I can be a verse or two written in the
life of you.

All flash fire and flame,
blazing when the tinderbox of your loneliness
catches with the nomadic spark of me.
Inevitably to only be dulled and dimmed
and turned to dust
with the ever flow of minutes and hours,
leaving only smoke and
toasted earth in our wake.

And yet...
yet...
maybe on this long and seemingly
endless winter night,
you find that you still want
to burn a little with me.

Our Chapter

Your lips move
but there is no sound.
Tunnel vision coming on,
I don't think I could stay even
if you asked me to.
I'll have to rewrite
my part in your story,
to some temporary and lesser role,
a small footnote in the life of you.
And maybe long from now,
you can remember
the small chapter of me,
of soul kisses
and summer heat.
I'll cradle all our truths
in some deep and muted place
and will hope that time,
for once,
will be kind.
You'll go on,
transcribing your veritable masterpiece,
and I'll raise my glass
to our few pages,
and find a kind of solace
in the knowledge that you were made
for far greater things than me.

Acceptance

Could you please
just be still for once,
and I'll lower my guards.
And finally,
there will be no more sounds uttered here,
quiet in the dark.
You can show me with your lips
and hands
what your voice can never convey,
and I will let go of all the hurt
and rest easy in your arms.
You can find a momentary peace
that always seems to elude you
in the haven of my embrace,
and I'll let you cage me
just for these moments
with your needs.
I won't say a word
if you don't say a word.
This is what we are.
The one true thing
you and I
have always been
and perhaps
will only ever be.

Tower of Babylon

Oh my love,
I could build the Tower of Babylon
with all the broken words
and promised lies.
I've burned at your pyre
for crimes that weren't mine.
I've opened all my veins
and let these past lives
bleed me dry.
Maybe someone,
someday,
can create something lovely
out of this mess,
stringing together our mistakes
like ocean pearls,
tied together in starlight.
Maybe then I can fade
into the black,
I can bathe in the white.

Humpty Dumpty

Oh Humpty Dumpty,
didn't you learn your lesson
well enough that last time?
Kept falling off of Life's walls
with no way to put back all your pieces.
Now you never fit quite right,
so many little cracks
for all your light,
all your love
to slip through.
And all the kings' men
still trample the earth
with your heart and innards
until only dust remains.
And yet, you keep plodding on,
broken little shell,
empty now of joy or pain,
leaking lost love
onto the empty ground.
Forever it seems you can be found
endlessly climbing walls
that will only,
inevitably,
break you once more.

The Middle

You don't like my questions,
I can't bear the lies.
Where does that leave us
except on opposing sides?

Simple truths, an easy fix;
I don't understand your hesitation.
You tear me down with doubts,
you chain me in devastation.
In lonely moments there seems
no chance at reconciliation...

Maybe if you reach for me
and I just reach for you,
we can find ourselves
somewhere in the middle,
someplace honest and true.

Victims

I'd close my eyes
but there is no safety there…
only memories that have claws
to drag you down shrouded roads
of a past that is better left unearthed.
I could get lost forever there,
a place where my skin is a
Pollock painting of black and blue.
Some days I can't rise from those depths,
it's easier to stay on the bottom,
lost among other shipwrecked victims
and their drowned lives.
Damaged skeletons and timber,
stagnant with age and
coated in silence.
Maybe there is an elusive peace
to be had here,
in the quiet of murky depths
of despair.
Maybe here I could sleep at last.

Memories

Down this long familiar road,
memories cascading over me.
I can no longer tell what are
real photographs in my head
and what are just rosy hued illusions
my mind has created of you.
I didn't know it was possible
for someone to feel this empty
and full of pain at the same time.
I see the store we'd visit after midnight,
the final red light before home,
the paths we used to walk.
I am haunted by our former life,
seeing parts of you in every stranger.
I don't want to hurt anymore...
please, if I ever mattered at all,
release me and let me be.

Bleach

Tiny flecks of snow,
a world gone quiet.
The busy city street on pause,
white-washed and silent,
distorted balls of colored lights and
a curtain of cold and flakes closing shut.
Everything looks brand new and oddly ageless
in the freshly fallen cornice blanket,
secret soft and dendrite star speckled.
Maybe if I stay still long enough
I can be covered, too...
reborn in ice,
blizzard white and wiped clean.
A little forlorn and hopeful snowman,
housed on a forgotten corner,
lost among glittering buildings,
blank and timeless.
Maybe someone will garnish me with a
rakish top hat or gift me with a
scarf the color of rainbows.
Or maybe I'll simply melt with the winter dawn,
mix in with the slush and the salt.
But for that brief moment,
I'll be bleached and unmarked,
whole again in the first flurry fall
of December,
softly glowing in the bleak light
of a solstice moon.

A Moment in Time

Banded lines from the window
and a stillness in the room,
the world outside these four walls,
muted and out of tune.

We breath in time and
mix our mingled air supply.
Limbs and emotions careless,
tangled and left to lie.

Once past the blindness of
passion and respite,
we struggle not to let our shutters down
and lose the newfound light.

A breaking of breathless promises;
small, ageless questions always intrude.
Uncharted waters to explore or
we simply drown in their latitude.

Do you feel it now?
Your soul seeking its way to mine?
Is this incessant or merely
a moment out of space and time?

Will you see more than I intend
if you look too close or too long?
Should we be content with the fleeting fervor
of this quick siren song?

Close your eyes and I'll keep my heart
from falling out of my pocket onto the floor.
Gather up belongings and wits,
I'll put my walls and ramparts back in store.

Bumping into awkward bodies and trained defenses,
we artlessly collide.
Lips caught for a moment quietly,
a love unbidden and untried.

Whisper soft and almost too sweet,
we'll taste perpetuity once again.
Bodies fused and spirits one,
and in this moment, forever without end.

Once in a While

Walking on these city streets,
keeping my eyes down,
each booted step punctuated by dead leaves
and broken colored glass.
Attempting to ignore shadows and strangers alike,
navigating the safest path,
even if it's ugly and littered and broken.
Someone's laughter makes me raise my gaze.
Fall foliage and tall brick buildings
outlined in black,
a lovely gray sky.
Bleak and beautiful.
My eyes collide with a passerby
and he bestows me with a crooked smile
and journeys past.
Maybe it's not so bad...
Maybe it's just perspective...
Maybe I just need to look up once in a while.

Cobwebs & Boxes

The smell of peat smoke and mountain air,
tasting of morning coffee and dew,
dancing bands of sunlight and clouds
marking their way across my skin.
I'll let the sounds of birdsong drown out
my troubled thoughts,
I'll lose myself watching the
diamonds glisten on cobwebs
by my feet from the night before.
Stubborn little things,
these small spiders,
remaking their silver, silken homes
again and again,
no matter how many times I displace them.
Maybe I am like a tiny spider,
obstinately remaking my home,
over and over again,
no matter how many times
Fate or acts of God or Nature
or clumsy people or even I destroy it.
Most days, I can pack away the sadness
into careful little boxes inside myself,
my giant warehouse
of broken and lost things.
But some days,
like today,
I can't seem to fold away the heartache
into neat laundry piles,

seal them away
with tape and string...
Today I am a creature on fire,
filled to the brim
with emotions that have names
that I have long since forgotten.
All this pain and joy
and sorrow seeping out,
like milk pouring from my pitcher
into the glass heart of me.
I am not sure if I am half empty
or half full...
I wish you could pull back my curtain,
take a peek inside,
and love all the lost things
hidden away there.
A raven call and new clouds halt these
empty tombs of thought,
for which I am grateful.
I'll get distracted instead by the
large expanse of open sky,
endless hills and valleys
and the unwritten stories that might lie there.
I see my small world narrow and
I am strangely comforted by my
comparative smallness,
enough to find the will to put it all away,
add it to another shelf
to be forgotten for a time.
Just clear my head and
empty my soul.

Maybe you know me just enough
to know all isn't quite right...
but for your sake,
we can both pretend
that there are no wounds,
nothing to forgive,
nothing to heal.
I will remain marked by all these cuts,
no matter what you refuse to see.
I am heavy with secrets,
laden with boxed emotions and ash.
Forged in fire,
I am soul-scarred.
Perhaps forever to be a warehouse of emotion,
hollowed out and packaged away,
gathering dust and tied with lonely heartstrings.

Raindrops

Blackened dreams and phantom hands
bring me back to the reality of our empty bed.
Some wounds run too deep,
some shadows can't be reached by the light.
The heavy clouds weep,
and I listen to the world outside this room
get washed away.
I follow the tear trails on your window pane,
each drop finding another to merge with
on its final descent to the earth.
Even raindrops find someone to fall with...
But maybe some damages can't be rectified,
maybe even Time can't fix all things.
I will never be enough,
broken pieces and a cracked heart.
I wonder if I join the downpour
if it would wash away all memory,
all thought.
Until all that remained was this
disjointed love and loss
I have for you,
lying in a quiet puddle outside your window
amongst the cold, wet earth
and the dark and weeping sky.

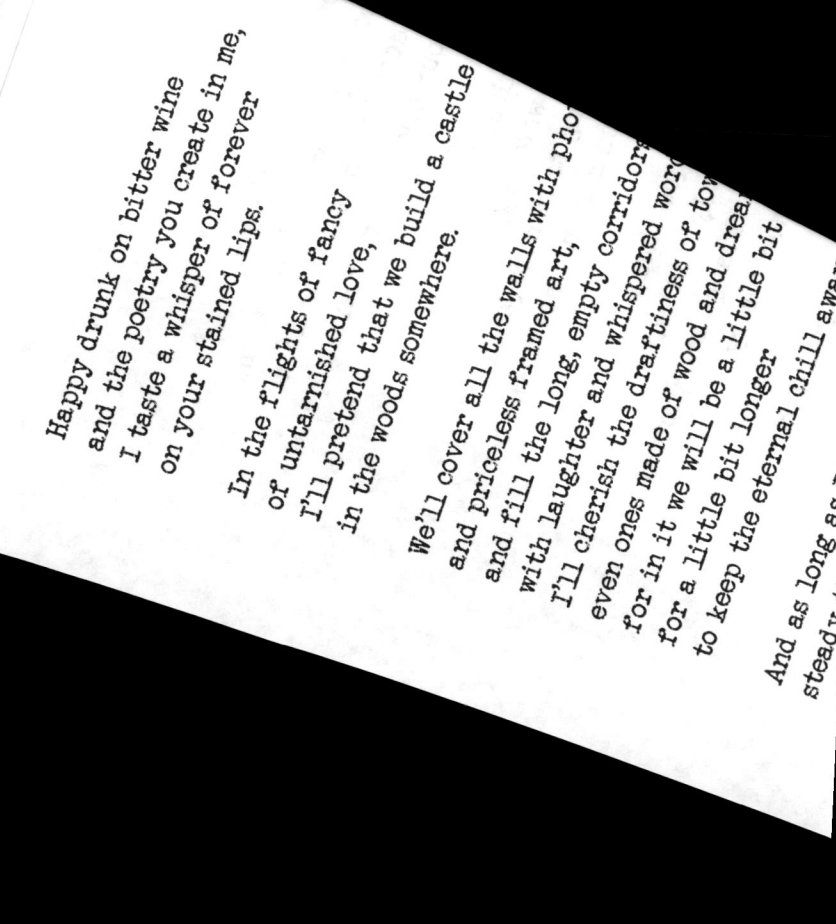

Maybe you know me just enough
to know all isn't quite right...
but for your sake,
we can both pretend
that there are no wounds,
nothing to forgive,
nothing to heal.
I will remain marked by all these cuts,
no matter what you refuse to see.
I am heavy with secrets,
laden with boxed emotions and ash.
Forged in fire,
I am soul-scarred.
Perhaps forever to be a warehouse of emotion,
hollowed out and packaged away,
gathering dust and tied with lonely heartstrings.

Raindrops

Blackened dreams and phantom hands
bring me back to the reality of our empty bed.
Some wounds run too deep,
some shadows can't be reached by the light.
The heavy clouds weep,
and I listen to the world outside this room
get washed away.
I follow the tear trails on your window pane,
each drop finding another to merge with
on its final descent to the earth.
Even raindrops find someone to fall with...
But maybe some damages can't be rectified,
maybe even Time can't fix all things.
I will never be enough,
broken pieces and a cracked heart.
I wonder if I join the downpour
if it would wash away all memory,
all thought.
Until all that remained was this
disjointed love and loss
I have for you,
lying in a quiet puddle outside your window
amongst the cold, wet earth
and the dark and weeping sky.

Happy drunk on bitter wine
and the poetry you create in me,
I taste a whisper of forever
on your stained lips.

In the flights of fancy
of untarnished love,
I'll pretend that we build a castle
in the woods somewhere.

We'll cover all the walls with photographs
and priceless framed art,
and fill the long, empty corridors
with laughter and whispered words.
I'll cherish the draftiness of towers,
even ones made of wood and dreams,
for in it we will be a little bit closer
for a little bit longer
to keep the eternal chill away.

And as long as I feel the
steady thrum of your heartbeat,
a safe and steady rhythm,
rising up from your skin to meet mine,
I can hold onto something
a little more real
than the rest of the world.

I can hope that maybe
I have found
my small slice of perfect,

Castle

A pair of meandering wanderers,
both seen too many miles of Life's highway.
Both with a deep fear of settling down,
we now find ourselves in an uncertain place.

I'm coffee-high and
you're people watching,
both pretending to be more jaded
than two hidden romantic hearts can be.

You'll ask the questions,
I'll answer in only riddles,
and together we'll laugh and pretend
through our former misery.

The sun spills across your face
like morning cream,
strong and clean and almost
more beautiful than I can bear.

I'll treat your pride like priceless china,
as you mock my hippie ways and
then kiss away the sting
until I lose my heart,
tumbling softly out of my chest
and into your waiting hands.

somewhere, somehow
in the dark and empty spaces
of your imperfections and mine.

All the tiny cracks that our light shines through
as endless as the horizon,
mayhap a home for two lost hearts
that can finally be
as constant and lovely as the dawn.

Life & Death

Small, little exhausted puffs of misted air
from my lungs,
my fingertips are fumbling and numb,
my heart is cold and heavy.
My thoughts keep circling around life and death,
endings and beginnings,
and all the stories bookended in-between.
Wild black and blueberries stain my boots,
a loud splash of color against
the decayed brown and leeched yellow
and faded orange autumn ground.
A pastel twilight background hints at me
between the tangled, twisted limbs
and the celery stalks of barren trees.
Even the silence is muted here,
punctuated only by the scurrying, unseen ghosts
amongst the littered, leafy floor
and thorny underbrush.
Such a swift and sudden end to a half finished life...
what tiny, finite flames
of light and breath we all are.
When did I see you last,
feel your skin on my skin?
Was it only a few hours ago?
A year? A lifetime?
Loss and loneliness skew the truth of memory,
love turns reality on its side.

I've spent too long in my thoughts,
the afternoon trail is now a shaded gray world
guarded by waving, wooded sentinels
and criss-crossed in shadows.
I make my way back to the harsh,
bright light of my dashboard,
and the familiar shape of my driver seat,
and put away all remaining questions into
that endless vault inside me.
I don't have any answers
but maybe we're not meant to.
I don't even know if I have
the right questions anymore.
Just moving from destination to destination,
room to room.
All I know for sure tonight
is that my movement,
for the sake of my sanity,
can't be back to you.

All That Remains

I'll read you poetry
that moves me
while you sleep next to me.
I want to give you all the words,
all the beautiful phrases and
lyrical prose ever written.
Pour it all from my mouth onto your skin,
let it soak into your bones and thought,
so that from time to time,
the letters will come leaking out,
reminding you of some lovely
rhyme or noun or place.
The pattern of my voice
beats in time with
the staccato of the autumn storm
outside our room.
We are cocooned in these four walls
with nothing but
breath and words,
with the heat of our combined bodies,
wrapped up like mummies,
entombed only in
flesh and silken sheets.
You look troubled,
even when you sleep.
I'll kiss the furrow of your worried brow and
whisper sweet nothings in your ear,
easing you back to a temporary peace.

These are the best of times,
when all else fades away,
and only you and I
and the rain
remain.

Open Road

Come and get a little lost with me,
just forget the world for a little while.
We can make our escape,
get in your car and distance ourselves,
mile by endless mile.

We can pretend that bad things
don't happen and that good people don't lie.
And that some things might last forever,
like these small eternities in these moments
between you and I.

My bare feet hanging out the passenger window
and you singing in tune with every radio song.
Hot summer air in our lungs,
I find myself staring at you with a love,
overwhelming and strong.

Two wooden hearts with roots starting to intertwine,
bound by something that looks steady and true.
Rather than just setting my heart on fire,
maybe instead you could plant it next
to the heart of you?

Could we just get lost out here on this open road,
build something from ashes, all shiny and new?
Could I be what you choose to keep and
could you love me like
I need you to?

Respite

Hush now, love.
Stand with me amongst the trees
and the falling snow
and the quiet.
Feel the heat of where you
and I collide,
and the contrast of the bite
of winter's breath
on your warmed neck.
Taste my breath
as it fogs into the air,
see the clarity of all that
we are together
in this moment only,
in the stillness here.
Some things are lasting,
some things are true
and deep
and real.
I'll lower my defenses
in this moment for you,
if you will do the same.
Allow us both to forget
the sins of yesterday,
mend all that has
been broken.
A snapshot of something
that looks and tastes
and feels like love,

that the Past will lie down
and be still for.
I'll leave a whisper soft kiss
on your cold lips,
and give you a small
gift of forever,
trapped perfect
in this memory for you.
You can close your eyes
and smell my skin
and take all that I am offering
inside you...
Let it heal your scars
and settle in your bones.
And know that even if you
open your eyes and
I am long since gone,
only mist and shadows
where I once was,
that you will always carry my heart
inside your chest,
wrapped tightly with yours,
tied together
for always and beyond.

Backroads & Eternity

An endless maze of twisted roads
lit by the twin beams of my headlights
and the glow I only see around you.
I see you close your eyes for a moment
in my passenger seat,
mentally questioning my driving skills,
your feet pressing imaginary pedals.
You crowd my compact space
with your body and your air
until every time I inhale
all I breath is you.
And you can't stop looking for dangers
around every curve of pavement,
while I can barely see straight,
distracted by your outline.
We laugh at random road names
and I push against the hard lines
of your comfort zone when I park us
in a random stretch of driveway and field.
You fiddle with interior lights
and worry over blind spots,
but my view is full of
the angular lines of your face,
sharp bones and full features.
All your shadows and planes,
speckled in starlight
that I know better than my own.
Suddenly I ache with a longing
I don't have the words for.

Your eyes,
dark and ever watchful,
meet the turbulent sea of mine,
and all the broken pieces
finally click into place.
And though I don't remember moving,
suddenly you are closer than before,
losing myself in lips and heat,
touching places somewhere
that kisses aren't supposed to reach.
You taste like waffle syrup and ice,
and I am lost to the ocean of you.
I won't fight this current,
I simply want to drown here.
And as you take me over,
with the gentle roughness of your hands
and the unmoving borders of your body,
our eyes meet and
no more words are needed.
Hot skin and cold winter air,
soft mouths and hard needs,
black night and shooting stars,
you and I will always be a combination
of the dark and the light.
And as we lay here
in the aftermath,
harsh breathing and spent bodies,
rapid heartbeats oddly loud and in sync,
I recognize that these suspended moments
might be all we ever have...

but as long as it is your face
filling my vision,
and your air in my lungs,
it will somehow have to be enough.
These perfect little eternities
written by us,
for only us to know and see.

Sirens

Sometimes I hear the sirens,
past and present,
and I ache somewhere deep inside myself,
a forgotten place.
Do you ever feel a longing rise up in you,
edged in regret,
bloodied with memory?
Do you ever wake wildly in the night
and reach for me
in the stillness,
in the dark?
Taste me on another's lips,
catch a glimpse of me
on a stranger's face
when you wish you weren't looking
but you somehow always are?
I hear those sirens
and I ache...
God, I ache for you.

Resting Place

Can't sleep...
the world tipped on its side.
The cold and my thoughts
weighing me down.
So heavy, I can't bear the
sound of silence...
Confusion settles in,
doubt creeps beneath my skin.
My own breath is too much
and too loud.
Could I just crawl inside you,
rest my weary head,
give everything away
and let it be?
You can kiss my eyelashes,
soothe my soul,
share some of my burdens
the same way
you share your blanket with me.
I'll be your resting place
and you can be mine,
even if it's just until the
morning light.

Someone to Choose Me

There is no moon tonight,
just humid air and
blood-red wine
and all the secrets that I keep.
My heart is a masochist,
full of a thousand needs for men
that never call
except for a place to sleep.

Is it even love if there's no exquisite pain?
Or have my many scars twisted my perception,
tilted my view?
Why is it that those I love
the hardest
always seem to bring me down,
never safe and never true?

They seem locked in
their own prison
of loving someone else,
it's never me that they choose.
Why does my skin need mapped
and my soul need to be touched
by someone that
I'll always lose?

Maybe pain, like love, needs to burn and quake,
so that if nothing else,
I know that I'm alive.
Maybe it's the bated breath, the unspoken hopes
that keep me returning and
help me to survive.

Just once under a moonless sky,
I want to find someone who sets
my body and my heart
to blaze.
Who can see only me and decide
that I am the one they want
not only for now,
but forever and always.

Death Among the Trees

Jumbled roots and
pine crushed dirt,
trees hug each other
like children,
swaying in time to
a song
I desperately want to hear.
Lay me down here
in this coffin of grass.
I'll lay so long
my body will feed the foxes
and my bones will remain
unearthed.
The white birches
can be my headstone
and the birds my
heavenly choir,
singing me gently into that
final sleep.
My canopy will by the
manic sky,
light to dark
and back to light again.
And even here,
in my wooded grave,
my every thought
will always be of you.

Old Friend

Ah, Loneliness...
my old and bitter friend.
It's been a while since we met,
forgotten for a time.
But as he wanders further
and further away,
I hear you knocking at my door,
waiting to be let in.
Ah, Loneliness...
my old and bitter friend,
here, alas,
we meet once again.

Beautiful & Broken Things

Oh shattered little shells
tossed by gray-green waves,
by forces so much greater than you.
I empathize with your sad and broken forms,
razor sharp edges and tiny cracks,
cutting without intent
any open skin that gets
too close to you.
Without purpose,
your half realized existence,
you lay forgotten,
overlooked in lieu of
shinier, unbroken versions.
But oh, I see all your
beauty and potential.
I'll gather you up
like precious diamonds,
lace you together like freshwater pearls,
string you along my neck like
the Crown jewels.
Each broken dip and rise of you,
catching the sun,
creating rainbows
everywhere the light touches.
Your jagged forms,
all flash fire
and color,
transformed by the air
and the brilliance of the sea.

The One

I have needs that could
swallow the world.
I have tears enough
to cover it in the sea.
I have a love that is
unending and true,
I just haven't found the one yet
who alone can set it free...

Halves to My Heart

I am so afraid I am breaking them,
these two little people.
That I am only showing them
what broken love looks like.
I tuck her fine hair behind her ear,
and cup my daughter's chin
in my hands,
and tell her that it's okay,
this is not what love is supposed to
look like anyway.
She looks so solemn sometimes,
grown up eyes,
shadowed and filled with her own secrets.
She tells me that she just wants
me to be happy,
and I feel my heart land in a jumbled mess
at her feet.
My little man tears up as he sees my attempt
to silence my weeping as I fold the laundry,
concentrating from sock to sock
with a kind of manic intensity
to stem the flow.
Such a soft and open heart,
he cuddles me and rests
his little head in the
nook of my shoulder.
He doesn't ask what's wrong or
who to blame,
he just wants to take my pain away.

When do we stop doing that?
Giving comfort and asking nothing in return?
I am humbled by my children's sweetness,
blanketed in their love.
I am suddenly ashamed
of my anguish,
pointless and constant.
He is gone.
As he always inevitably is,
for he never remains for very long.
And yet here, I have two little perfect
halves to my heart,
staring up at me,
reminding me what real love looks like.
And I want to explain to them
that they are enough,
but somehow I can't find the syllables,
the words get stuck in my throat.
I can only hope it is conveyed
in my embrace,
as I wrap them up
with my arms,
small heads on each shoulder.
I pray they can feel what my mouth
cannot seem to convey,
that they have been the only two
great loves of my life,
past, present and for always.

Last Call

Dim lit rooms and long bar line,
we gather at the trough.
Cattle to the call,
slave to the whiskey bell.
Shuffling feet, averted eyes,
alone in these crowds.
Married only to another tumbler
of ice and fire,
no words are wanted here.
Burning all the way down,
settling in the core,
little seeds of warmth
branching out to every limb,
it's both our every breath
and our lonely demise.
Little lives,
little deaths.
A taste of heaven
burnt by a little hell.
We give up our keys
but we leave our chains
tied to our chairs.
There are worse ways to go,
worse ways to live, by far.
We numb the pain of memories
with a liquid balm,

one long chain gang,
held together by our desire
to be lost
coupled with our need to be found.
Our true stories get lost
in the amber water,
without purpose,
without sound.
Heading inevitably towards
the final Last Call,
the merciless passage of time.
Please just make one more
for the road,
to fill all the empty spaces,
so for a moment only
we can be
stirred and
strangely profound.

A Chance of Storms

I do not know the future...
I cannot see beyond this current
place we find ourselves.
But just as the Moon knows
the shape of the Ocean,
the give
and the take,
the high
and the low surge of waves,
the endless depths
and the curling wake,
all the intimate layers
of salt and darkness,
brine and air,
water and light.
That is how I know you.
The future may remain
shrouded in mist and
lost to mystery,
but no matter which phase we are,
with you there is always
a chance of storms.
Immense and otherworldly,
you destroy ships
and souls
and shorelines.
That remains known to me,
as true and as certain
as the moonlit tide.

Dreams

Pine smoke fills the frosted air,
I taste of Pinot Noir
and hidden things.
This is what dreams taste like.
Shadows and firelight
making a thousand masks
on my face,
I am no one
and everyone at the same time.
You lose me
to the night.

Simple Things

Morning dew and honeysuckle
make me yearn for simple things...
Maybe I'll find a lonely tree
in a forgotten meadow,
and I'll lay down my roots
and my blanket can be the canopy of leaves
and stars,
and the wind will be
my lonely song.

Twilight

I breathe in the night air,
cool and damp with early harvest showers
and tendrils of late summer humidity.
The evening whispers to me
in the drones of insects
and secrets.
Sleep eludes me...
The dusk is too loud.
I am too alive,
my skin stretched too tight.
I'll go merge with the
hum of locusts and the
shadows of twilight.

Midnight Circus

Come and see my twilight circus,
tents of shimmering black and
lined with silver,
streamers of starlight catching and throwing shadows
and glittered slices of the moon
whenever the clouds break.

You've come to see the show,
just like all the others,
tickets are sold out and so few.
I'd tell you to take a seat but tonight,
like every night,
is standing room only.
Stay still and remain quiet,
and remember, no photos, please.

Every act is coated in enchantment,
distorted by the late night shapes that constantly
cross the center stage,
telling their own secrets and stories,
seen out of the corner of everyone's eyes,
but understood by none.

Amongst the parade of loud costumes
and heavy spotlights
and intentional misdirections,
there are still
grains of truth

to be found here
if you know where to look,
lost in the color and
drowned out in the noise.

Taste all the candied offerings,
salty and luscious and sweet,
filling up all the emptiness in you
but leaving a dryness in your throat
that never truly leaves.

There are no nets for the trapeze artists,
the bejeweled clowns don top hats
and the lions all have diamond teeth.
The ring leader does not take center stage,
but rather hides behind the scenes.

You are coated in stardust and popcorned revelry,
you are blinded by rows of stringed lights
and heavy canvas.
You trade a little part of yourself,
unknown and keenly felt,
before the last tent flap closes.

Alas, the show must end,
as all things must do,
powered down and packed up.
You are almost unsure it was really there,
beckoning you closer,
selling tickets of mirrored gold,
giving glimpses of

all the dark magic
you can only find in the
hidden corners of the world.

With the harsh light
of morning and the loss of sugar highs
and the mystique that only nighttime can bring,
all the false fanfare and the beauty
seems now only a half remembered dream...
for isn't that what we all are?
Just unknown spaces that can be glimpsed,
lost somewhere between
what is real and what is fantasy.

Flash Flame

Moments that echo
far past what we say is real...
You are the fire,
I am the kindling.
I want to be more
than a flash flame.
I want more than quick coffees
and participation ribbons,
I want more than a
"rebounded" second place.
But sometimes "more" is also
more than I can take.
So instead
just be quiet,
be still.
Make the choice
to just savor the night with me.
Then we can say our well wishes
and we can part as strangers
or friends
or something we both wish
we could be.

World Eater

Skin-walker...
Trying on different lives,
never comfortable in your own blood and bones.

Truth-peddler...
Selling stories and dreams,
glass bottles that turn to dust in your hands.

Storm-bringer...
wind and rain in your touch,
black clouds on your brow and thunder and
lightning on your lips.

World-eater...
Consuming all the light and dark,
all the love and pain,
the sea and the sun.

You are the enigma of all these things and more...
and yet, somehow still lovely to me.

Are you instead the ocean,
endless, dark, and deep...
That carries the dance of sunlight
just under the surface,
life hidden in the curl of the waves,
only to be seen if I would choose
to look beneath?

Or are you the black hole in the cosmos,
also endless, dark, and deep...
That draws everything and everyone
around you into your abyss,
consuming all mind and heart and spirit,
until there is nothing left of me?

Unlikely Companions

Alas, the glorious wreckage
when two unlikely worlds collide...

You arrive 15 minutes early,
I consider it a good day
if I am only 15 minutes late.

You have balances and spreadsheets
and this mysterious phenomenon called a budget,
I don't know the current amount in my bank account
and blatantly ignore the low numbers
of my credit score.

You are up early in the morning
with your checklists in hand
and on the go as the sun rises,
I wake at noon and do most of
my best work after 2 AM.

You smile for every photo
and thrive in the center of it all,
I hide from every camera lens
and would rather melt into the background
if I could.

You rhyme in your poetry
with clear stanzas and hopeful undertones,

I have no rhythm or reason
to the madness that I write
in long lines of sadness and questions and loss.

You yearn for long glances and eye contact
and drawn out silences to contemplate,
I get nervous when you look at me
and need to fill the quiet with
a steady stream of nonsense.

You talk of forever and love
and wear your heart on your sleeve,
I shy away from labels and promises
and turn a blind eye to the potential
stirrings of my soul.

Maybe that is the power and the apex of it all,
that despite all of our differences,
love still gives us all
a common ground and
binds that tie.
It makes all the glare of
our disparities glitter like
crystals in daylight,
throwing prisms of color
and hope and life.

New York

Sharp edges and clean lines,
a landscape of rises and plateaus,
sudden shots of sunlight with seemingly endless
pockets of shadow around every corner turn.
Fur coats and red bottomed heels standing next
to old newspapers and bodies swathed in
dirty blankets,
this city is painted only in contrasts.
Angry bursts of car horns
harmonizing with siren wails,
shouts and coughs and chatter,
a constant drone of humanity
coating every particle of air,
making the oxygen
a little harder to breathe up here.
A patchwork swarth of faces,
even people watching
takes extra effort,
eyes and noses and cheekbones
bleed into the next,
until it's all just wave after wave
of unseen flesh and blood and bone
covered in winter coats and skin.
How do they connect up here?
Or is it just a city of loneliness,
strangers chasing solitary dreams,

all lined up in boxes,
Starbucks in one hand,
cellphone in the other?
I am on a safari of sorts,
observing and awestruck by long legs
and lean profiles,
a little frightened at the prospect of
getting lost in
the glare of these neon lights or
crushed by the neverending
loop of sound.
Like a dreamscape,
this city feels a little unreal,
all the edges blurred by the veneer of
superficial prosperity
to cover up all the sadness,
just a layer down,
under the glitzy surface.
Maybe the only world we see is just
a reflection of ourselves...
Some can look at this
maze of avenues and skyscrapers
and see only possibilities in the mirrored walls
and cobblestone streets.
What does it say about me that
I feel as though I have already
OD'd on humanity
after a few short hours here and
already long for a
quiet and dark place to escape to?

Tree-lined and silent,
an unfettered sky filled with air
my heavy lungs can actually breathe.
But promises have been made
and friendships to keep,
so I'll join the throng of herded people,
melt into the crowded sidewalk,
blending in with the loud chaos
and flashing lights and
discordant symphony of sounds
to get lost along with the
masses of humanity
on these parallel streets.

Lost & Found

Your eyes are kind
and your hands are sure,
even when your voice
always has questions.
Your touch is pure amnesia,
making all memories
fade away in the
presence of you.

I could get lost here
in these four walls,
in the disarray of these blankets
and the sounds you make
when I run my fingers
on your skin,
flesh to flesh.

Small soul touches and
full bodied vintages,
our story unfolds somewhere
between my words
and your darkened rooms.

You are lovely
and unsure,
yet familiar in a way that
something in the center
of me recognizes you.

It calls to something forgotten in me,
that well of words I threw into the abyss long ago,
better left untouched and unknown.

You draw from my ground water,
you drink heavy and deep,
heart drunk on something
you want to acknowledge but
I am too afraid to voice.
I don't know what
the dawn will bring,
all harsh light and muted edges,
smoke and mist and
flush colored mystery.

But I do know
I don't want to leave
the safe encampment of your arms,
nor the steady rhythm
of your heartbeat,
thrumming against my cheekbone.

Maybe morning and
all its pesky questions
can wait...
stay just beyond the horizon.
And we can stay
trapped in this moment,
both lost and found,

life-weary and bodies fused,
waiting for answers
that might never come.

If these moments are all
we ever have,
please know they have
etched tattoos on my skin,
small worlds and memories,
surreal and profound.

It's already more
than most people will ever have,
here in the dark,
lasting forever in the
penned lines of my poetry
and the silver lining of our hearts.

Oceans

You are not my usual cup of tea,
and I am not your normal style,
and yet,
we fit together like oceans and shorelines,
submerged and buried,
ebbing and flowing.
No definitive lines,
just earth and water and air.
I recognize and know better now,
I see the world catcalling your senses,
the glimmer that surrounds your vision.
Your dreams are bigger than mine,
there is only room for one in the
sidecar of your life.
Instead of fighting against what is,
despairing over what cannot be,
I'll draw you in for another
high tide,
let our bodies writhe and ache,
let you drown for another moment
in me,
while I lay easy for a breath
amongst your sand and
the merging of our sea.

Loneliness of a Friend

You always show up
like a set of keys I once lost,
random and welcome,
a little necessary and yet tarnished by
the passage of time.

Like a handwritten letter from
a childhood friend,
unexpected and lovely,
inspiring a dichotomy of emotions,
reconnecting but unsure anymore
of the right way to respond.

Though you have more lines
on your face each time,
just as I do,
the scent of you remains unchanged by years,
woodsmoke and cigarettes,
long summer evenings and
unbridled yearnings by twilight.

Your hands are still
strong and sure,
but there are entire
new landscapes of sadness
in your eyes,
a slowness in your step
that I don't recall.

The world is an easy place
to forget the foundations of yourself,
one day waking up older
but not wiser,
more aged and yet somehow more lost.

I am not even sure why
the sight and touch of you
still makes me want to
heal some of your wounds,
ease some of your apparent
loneliness in these moments.

Even though I don't understand
it myself,
I'll still lie here in the
mottled purple and blue
of dawn with you.
Desperate for coffee and answers,
but innately not wanting
to diminish the shallow web
of intimacy we have spun
in the dark.

So instead I will just
taste and feel and give,
but only just enough.
For while it soothes the ache,
time with you remains
inevitably fleeting and
quickly gone.

But I have learned the hard way
to accept all the things
and people and situations
I cannot change.
Instead I will be grateful
for a moment of realness,
no matter how brief,
in a fake and empty world
that these stolen minutes
with you create.

Strange Times

Smokescreens and misdirection,
angry mobs and ongoing division,
every line on the internet seems
coated with angst and rage.
I never wanted my children to grow up
in a world so full of hate.
Whether paper masks or just
a different filtered face,
we are slowly becoming
watered-down versions of ourselves,
jumping from bandwagon to bandwagon,
societal sheep being herded by
each new headline.
When did we forget
The Golden Rule,
when did questioning begin
to equate bigotry,
or thinking differently translate
to unacceptance?
How can a world that is focused solely
on the glittering surface
ever appreciate the realness
I have tattooed on my soul,
all the unique scars we each carry,
the hard earned qualities that
can only be found when we as humans
dig deep in ourselves and each other?

Blue lights and small screens,
oddly voyeuristic and filled with
knee-jerk judgements,
we are somehow more seen
but less connected than ever before.
I want my young ones to be
their wondrous, glorious selves,
unmasked and all too real,
pursuing truth and magic equally,
looking for wonder in every moment,
finding beauty in every person and every place.
To be courageous and yet tempered with grace,
strong in their convictions and
yet gentle in spirit.
Therefore my little willows,
despite living in a forest of deception,
I pray will have deep roots that
will keep them grounded,
learning how to bend when it's needed but
with trunks and souls this world
can never break.

Letting Go

Partings are like my morning coffee,
oh so necessary and bittersweet.
And I have never much liked endings...

Like the last page of a favorite book,
or the last leaf of autumn falling to a cold earth.
But alas, novels must have their final lines and
the first snow of winter
inevitably must settle in.

Saying goodbye,
letting go...
it is the required cracking and
breaking of our souls,
making room for
light and growth,
new meetings and adventures.

It is a fundamental truth,
but somehow even knowing this,
it doesn't make it easier to bear,
nor lesson the pain.

Like spring taxes or
the relentless aging of my body or
the damn alarm I need to set
in order to wake up at dawn,

I am always wishing it away.
To hold off a little longer in
the untethering of ties
that the heart of me
knows I need to break.

Somehow I'll find the strength
to say farewell,
to read the last words,
and make angels in the solstice snow.
And accept the sidewalk cracks
under the surface of me.

For I can no longer be
static and small...
I have to say goodbye
in order to finally breathe.

Metamorphosis

Bones grinding and reshaping,
layers and masks peeled away
and replaced,
a metamorphosis of the soul.

The winds of change
are so oft like a tornado,
leaving wreckage and waste,
only skeletons and fallen frames
of a former existence
in its wake.

Shedding old ways and
former habits,
painstaking and arduous,
layer by layer,
all that has been forgotten
or hidden away,
until I am the only thing
that remains.

My new feet are clumsy
with the steps of this dance,
my lips feel strange
when they taste the shape
of untried words,
my mind stumbles down these
unknown and untraveled
trails of thought.

Vulnerable and unsure,
all the best laid plans of yesterday
are now broken on the floor.
Standing among the shards and debris,
for once,
rather than forging ahead,
cutting against the sharp edges
of a shattered former life,
I'll choose to remain unmoving
for a time.

So that not even the gales of history
nor temptations of tomorrow
will move me.
For I am beginning to comprehend
what I need to hold on to,
what foundations I should build.
And all the things that I need to release,
people and places and patterns
that I need to let go of,
in order for me to breath
and grow.
I will have learned how to bend,
but I will no longer break.

I'll just feel the air in my lungs,
and relearn the lines of me
until I can love all of them.
I'll learn to be steady.
I'll choose to be true.
I'll just be me.

Home

Moments like these
I can't stem the words
flooding out of me,
pouring from some deep well inside.
Syllables running down my finger bones,
splashing ink and blood on the page.
They bleed me dry,
a creature of loss and agony,
twisted and despairing.
I am brought back by the twin flames
in the distance,
both compass and map,
cutting across the dark.
Remembering perhaps
all is not truly lost.
That I might be a small boat
on a large ocean that seems
endless and abysmal,
lonely and deep.
But if I keep following
the beams of my
little lighthouses,
bright beacons in the gloom,
I will find my way
to safer waters
and a familiar shore.

Past bays of shipwrecked memory
and unseen sea monsters and
underwater dangers,
and all the way to the
warmth of little arms
and the light of home.

Free

I wish I could wear my scars
like diamonds,
and care less about what others
might see.

Some days I just need soft hands
and a patient soul
that can sit in the gloom and in
the quiet with me.

Maybe then I could be more than
just an empty vessel,
a reservoir for others' needs and expectations,
their own loss and misery.

And in that slow unfurling of time,
balanced and steady,
we can exchange the broken pieces of ourselves,
finally known and truly free.

Acknowledgments

The most sincere thank you to all of my family and friends who have been forced to read my words and listen to my angst innumerable times, and yet remained constant with their support and feedback.

Demi Stevens, thank you for all your incredible patience and input.

And a heartfelt thank you to Heather and Randy, my chosen family, for all the comfort, support, and all things "prickly and hard to eradicate."

And finally to all those who have loved me or broken me or both over the years... all these words remain yours.

About the Author

Chelsea True is a poet, a photographer, a wishful artist, and a dreamer who suffers from short bouts of realism. Her favorite way of passing the time is with her two favorite people, Zoë and Chase, and her fur baby, Bullet. Chelsea is a self-proclaimed geek, who shamelessly pours ridiculous amounts of hours into gaming, books, and entertainment. She resides in the wilds of Pennsylvania and continues to write as often as her soul demands.

www.ingramcontent.com/pod-product-compliance
Lightning Source LLC
Chambersburg PA
CBHW071504080526
44587CB00014B/2204